T0118603

Perceptions *Of* African **American** Women **About** *Their* Dietary **Habits**

Christine Dial-Benton, Ph. D.

Doctor of Philosophy Degree specializing in
Exercise, Health and Fitness

Order this book online at www.trafford.com
or email orders@trafford.com

Most Trafford titles are also available at major online book retailers.

Printed in the United States of America.

ISBN: 978-1-4669-5424-3 (sc)
ISBN: 978-1-4669-5426-7 (hc)
ISBN: 978-1-4669-5425-0 (e)

Library of Congress Control Number: 2012915463

Trafford rev. 08/22/2012

 www.trafford.com

North America & international
toll-free: 1 888 232 4444 (USA & Canada)
phone: 250 383 6864 ♦ fax: 812 355 4082

Table of Contents

Abstract

This study begins with a review of the lifestyles of the diet and health of African American ancestors. It then takes us through the nutritional impact of generations of slavery, in which most of African families were fed the scraps of the animals and plants. Unfortunately, even today many African families cherish those foods, which contribute to heart disease and hypertension.

The U.S. Department of Agriculture (USDA) has conducted food consumption surveys since the 1930's. These surveys provide an up-to-date picture of the dietary status of Americans, how much they are eating at home or away, and the degree to which they are meeting dietary recommendations. Surveys such as this are very limited in the study of African American women's dietary habits. This known fact plus the fact that the writer is an African American woman is what inspired this study on the dietary habits of African American women.

The review of literature discusses topics such as African Americans health during the slavery era, post-emancipation African American health, historic African American health initiatives, present limitations on African American health, focus on African American women, present health problems facing African American women and factors affecting the health of African American women. From these topics there are discussions such as factors destroying contemporary African Americans. Among the factors are stress, poor diet, general distrust of the medical establishment, poverty, physiological differences, obesity and unawareness of health issues.

A geographically uniform diverse group of African American women were surveyed concerning their dietary habits. This survey reviews current thinking, attitudes and dietary habits of African American women.

The survey was a multiple-choice questionnaire of fifteen items. A wide range of issues regarding the intake of the recommended daily allowance for vital nutrients was explored. As a result of information gained in the present study, the writer suggest that more research of this type should take place. The writer also recommends that African American women of all ages, income and educational level view their diet as a serious issue and put forth a stronger effort to prevent poor dietary habits.

Introduction

Recent years have seen a tremendous growth in scientific knowledge of the relationship between diet and health. This increase in knowledge has informed dietary recommendations to promote health. It has also started a campaign to educate Americans on more healthful eating habits. (Guthrie, Derby and Levy, 1994).

American consumers show a high level of awareness of the relationship between their diets and serious diseases such as heart disease and cancer. (Derby and Fein, 1995). Public health campaigns, along with growing media attention to diet and health topics have raised awareness among less educated as well as the more educated consumers (Ippolito and Mathios, 1996).

This study will provide an up-to-date picture of the degree to which three groups of African American women are meeting dietary recommendations. The women in the study will be grouped according to age, income and education. They will complete a survey concerning their dietary habits. This study was designed in hopes that it would contribute to the evolving literature concerning the factors that promote general poor health among African American women.

As the literature review will show, there is ample documentation of the health problems faced by the African American community in general and by African American women in particular. Issues regarding health promotion among African American women have not been adequately researched.

There have been a number of important studies, many of which will be discussed below. These are important studies, which have been undertaken, in the past few years that have significant gaps in knowledge. Troubling questions are also present. For example, as Randall (1993) suggests, since hypertension has different causes for African American women, how do we know that the health promotion regimes that have been shown to work for White and/or male hypertension patients will be as effective for African American women?

A few recent research projects (e.g., Maridee & Jones, 1996; Sanders, Phillips, 1996; and Nies, Vollman, & Cook, 1999) have attempted to identify correlates of health promotion activities among African American women, but much remains to be learned in this area. These projects represent the first phase in an ongoing research project aimed at adding to existing knowledge about factors influencing the health and fitness of African American women.

In brief, the study reported in this paper entails a survey of a sample of African American women concerning key areas related to the perception about their dietary habits. The literature addresses the historical patterns and traditional role played in the family by African American women.

Purpose Of The Study

The purpose of the study is to determine how the three variables (age, income and level of education) may interact with African American women's perceptions of their own dietary habits. The writer selected this topic for her Project Demonstrating Excellence (PDE) because of her longstanding interest in the issue of African American women's health in being related to their dietary habits. The writer is an African American woman and has been aware since grade school of the particular stresses and health challenges faced by African American women. Black women seemed to be always taking care of everyone else's health and diets, often neglecting their own.

As an adult, the writer has had an abiding interest in African American women's health and diet issues. Pursuing this project has enabled her to learn more about the causes and effects of ill health as it is related to dietary habits among African American women. The writer intend to continue this learning process, eventually preparing a book-length manuscript for and about African American women. In the discussion section below, the writer identifies some of the weaknesses in the study reported in this paper. She intends to replicate this study using a larger and more representative sample of African American women as well as additional survey questions. The writer will include the results of that replication in the book.

The book will also include useful information not only about dietary habits but also health care, disease and health promotion activities such as exercise. The writer intends to convey her knowledge that good dietary habits causes good health which is more than just being not ill. If the dietary habits are good then there will be good health, which involves a balance between body, mind, and spirit. African American women deserve such good health. The writer hope to join the ranks of the African American women who have come before her in promoting the individual and institutional changes needed to make health in its fullest sense the norm among African American women. The writer will be looking at the dietary habits of these women to promote the change.

Research Question

What is the perception of a selected sample of African American women about their dietary habits?

Statement of the Problem

The literature indicates that age, income and the level of education may be among the factors contributing to the general poor health of African American women. However, it gives little information about African American women's perceptions on how these three variables interact with their own health.

According to research, in the United States today, approximately 52 percent of African American women are obese compared with 32 percent of White women. From information gained in the literature of this study, dietary habits play a major role in the obesity of African American women. Obesity can cause hypertension, which is a major risk factor for coronary heart disease. Hypertension infringes upon the health of African American women much more than it does upon the health of women in other groups. (Public Health Services, 1995).

Literature Review

Nutrition and Diet

The U. S. Department of Agriculture (USDA) has conducted food consumption surveys since the 1930's. The surveys provide an up-to-date picture of the dietary status of Americans, how much they are eating at home or away from home and the degree to which they are meeting dietary recommendations.

The Continuing Survey of Food Intake by Individuals (CSFII) surveys provided information on the percentage of individuals consuming specific foods. Overall, 83% of American ate some type of vegetable on any given day in 1994. One-fourth ate fried potatoes, including French fries or potato chips. Only 9% ate a dark-green vegetable and only 13% ate a deep-yellow vegetable. Over half of all Americans ate some type of fruit or drank fruit juice on any given day in 1994.

CSFII survey shows that vitamin intake is high among most age groups. The intake of certain minerals remains to be a problem. The average 1-day intake for all age groups exceeded the Recommended Dietary Allowance (RDA) for protein, vitamin A, C, B-12, thiamin, riboflavin, niacin, folate and phosphorus. Intake above the RDA's do not mean that everyone consumes an adequate amount, nor do they tell how many people are meeting RDA's.

Studies have found that perceptions of the ability to regulate health through diet and nutrient intake vary across income and racial strata (Block, Rosenberger, and Patterson; Block and Subar, Rose, 1997). Studies have also shown that nutrient consumption patterns vary similarly. Studies comparing dietary habits of African Americans and Whites often have conflicting results. For example, Block and Subar, Block et al., and Swanson conclude that African Americans consume less fat than do Whites. In contrast, Patterson found that African Americans consume more fat than do other population groups. Similar inconsistencies are also found in studies of dietary diversity. Although dietary differences between African Americans and Whites may be ambiguous, Stevens, Kumanyika, and Keil reported that the rate of obesity in African American women is roughly twice that of White women. Perceptions of weight were also found to differ significantly among the two groups, with overweight White women reporting lower satisfaction with their weight than did overweight African American women. With respect to income, Lutz, Blaylock, and Smallwood reported income—related differentials in food consumption patterns. Low-income and higher-income households were found to have reduced fresh vegetable consumption by 22%, in the periods 1977-78 and 1987-88. Tippett also found lower fruit and vegetable consumption in lower-income households. Basiotis showed that vitamin C and protein had high-income elastic ties. Considering the relatively high price of citrus and meat products, low-income households could hardly afford these products and associated nutrients.

Differentials among various socioeconomic and demographic subgroups have been documented in nutrient intake, in health status, and in perceptions about the role of nutrition in health. However, it is important to understand the relationship between health awareness and dietary intake for various socioeconomic and demographic subgroups. In conclusion it was indicated that individuals in all groups who were skeptical about health recommendations, diet-disease risk, and popular views about weight and health tended to consume less healthy diets. This suggests that convincing people of the benefits of adequate diet can enhance proper dietary intakes. Perceptions about the relationship between health, weight, and nutrition seem not to have positive impacts on nutrition for minorities and low-income individuals, whereas they did impact nutrient intake for other consumers. This suggests that merely educating the minority and low-income subgroups without addressing their income limitations or other socioeconomic reasons for differentials may be inadequate. However, the finding that more specific diet-disease knowledge seems to contribute to a healthier diet for all groups suggests that the most effective method of nutritional education is to highlight the disease element of poor nutrition. (Tippett,1994)

Shiriki K. Kaymanyika is a noted expert on obesity in minorities. She shared insight into her research at several lectures in 1997. Her research has found that the African American woman's poor weight management is more than lack of self-control. Kuymanyika found that obesity in African-American women is independent of socioeconomic status. She stated that there are cultural aspects to obesity in African American women. Having a heavy figure is more desirable in the African American community than in other communities. Events are often centered around food with African Americans. Overall, African American women make less money and have poorer access to health care than their White counterparts. Many women, who have trouble losing weight, often cite the expense of healthier foods as the reason.

Kuymanyika found that people were surprised to find that poor African Americans ate better than rich Whites back in the 1960's. We have changed the definition of what is a healthy diet. A healthy diet is a poor person's diet, it's a Third World country's diet. It's rice and beans. It's the unprocessed foods that have large quantities of starch, and complex carbohydrates, a little bit of meat for flavor, a little bit of fat and a lot of vegetables. Back in the old days that is what we had available to eat, and today we are trying to acquire status with steak. (Ethnic News-Watch@Softline Information, Inc. 1990).

Another study done by the Alabama Department of Public Health in 1993, revealed that low-income conditions, due to an individual unique living situations will influence ones health perceptions and behaviors. The study included both African and European American low-income women.

Women were asked their beliefs about the need for exercise and ways, if any, that they themselves exercise. This enabled the identification of their personal behavior in certain areas as well as the barriers and facilitators to health promotion. Forty-nine women took part in the study. Fifty-two percent (52%) were African American and forty-three percent (43%) were married. Thirty percent (30%) of the women completed Junior high school, and forty-one percent (41%) had a high school education. Four percent (4%) of participants reported that they had no formal education and thirteen percent (13%) reported that they had completed elementary school. The mean age was 48 years with a range of 18 to 86.

Forty-six percent (46%) of women responded that they barely made ends meet. Thirteen percent (13%) reported that they did not have enough money to pay bills. Thirty-five percent of women indicated they had enough monet to pay bills with little left over each month.

African American Health During the Slavery Era

Few accounts of African American history include attention to the health status of African Americans under slavery. Survival itself was clearly the most important health issue for enslaved Africans. Slave traders had little concern for the welfare of their human cargo, choosing instead to overload their vessels, assuming that many lives would be lost in the course of the brutal passage from Africa to the Americas (Bennett, 1982). Upon arrival, circumstance were somewhat different, as the potential market value of the slaves led the slave traders to pay close attention to their health status. Most slaves were sold based on their physical assets and abilities, with health being a major criterion (Mitchell, 1944). Slave owners had some concern for the health and survival of their slaves, because they were seen as property. However, slave narratives indicate that the provisions made by slave owners for the health of their slaves varied widely. Some owners guarding their investments by providing substantial food and health care while others were known to starve their slaves and literally work them to death. Most owners provided at least minimal health care, often delegating slaves to serve as doctors or midwives to other slaves. In the period preceding and following the Civil War, the argument that slave owners provided good living conditions for their slaves because they were economically motivated to do so became common among supporters of slavery but this was by no means generally true. Similarly, supporters of slavery claimed that people of African descent had no concern for their own health or ability to care for themselves and would surely perish were the protections offered by slavery removed (J.H. Jones, 1993). Slaves had little control over the conditions of their lives and had little opportunity to better their health. However, slaves certainly were not passive in the face of the many challenges to their health that slavery represented. Given the slightest opportunity to do so, slaves enhanced the nutrition available to them by gardening *(often with seeds brought over from Africa)* and hunting or fishing. In addition, slaves adapted traditional methods of herbal healing to the natural resources of the land in which they found themselves. Recipes for cures and tonics devised by slaves were passed along from generation to generation, surviving well into the post-emancipation era (Hurston, 1990).

The diseases common among slaves were not very different than those that were common among the general population at the time. However, mistreatment, malnutrition, lack of health care, and insufficient clothing and shelter certainly increased the vulnerability of slaves to disease. Working conditions varied with the temperament of the owner, as did the use of physical punishments such as whipping. Such physical punishments represented health risks because they were traumas to the body and created the conditions for infection.

Until recently, it was common for the medical profession to blame slaves for their ill health by citing poor sanitation or hygiene practices (e.g., Clark, 1941). Such attitudes towards the health practices of African Americans were caused by and helped to maintain the racist attitudes of the medical profession (J.H. Jones, 1993). In reality, the fact that slaves had little *access* to proper hygiene and sanitation facilities was probably one of many factors contributing to ill health among enslaved African Americans.

Post-Emancipation African American Health

Reconstruction represented a period of both positive change and frustration for African Americans in the South following the Civil War. Many of the minimal health care systems on which slaves had relied had been destroyed or disrupted in the course of the war. Migration and dislocation must have separated many former slaves and free people of color from the local traditional healers on whom they had relied. While supporters of slavery claimed that the loss of plantation-based health care would be hurtful to former slaves, the failure of the national government to provide former slaves with economic compensation did much more damage. Freedman's Bureaus provided some health services, but these were short-lived. By the end of the Reconstruction era, lands and the fruits of slave labor had been returned to the hands of the former slave owners, leaving most former slaves in abject poverty. The health of these former slaves began to deteriorate. Those who had promoted slavery argued that this meant they had been right. By the turn of the twentieth century, many physicians, anthropologists, and popular writers had come to view emancipation as a veritable death sentence for blacks (J.H. Jones, 1993, p. 20).

In the post-Reconstruction period, many former slaves again turned to their peers for health services based on traditional methods such as herbalism. F.A. Jones (1900) reported the use of folk remedies to drive out diseases, deriding such remedies. The efficacy of such services may be debated. Medical doctors have traditionally condemned natural medicine and condemned the spiritual practices of others as superstition. More recently, ethnobotanists have pointed out that modern medicine like aspirin and digitalis are derived from plants originally identified as curative by traditional healers. The likelihood is that some of the cures offered by non-medical healers were effective while others were not.

Regardless of the efficacy of the non-medical treatments utilized by former slaves, the fact remains that former slaves had little access to the level of health care that had become standard for non-impoverished white citizens. There were some African Americans who had received formal or informal training in the medical arts, but these were few. Thus most African Americans were forced to seek services from white physicians.

As a result of a combination of factors including lack of economic resources, refusal by some white physicians to treat black patients, and the rise in scientific medicine, African Americans were more often objects of study than subjects of treatment (F.A. Jones, 1900).

Frequently, the medical research performed on African Americans had the primary aim of demonstrating their mental or physical inferiority. Further, there were many White medical researchers who did not see African Americans as fully human. The research practices to which they were subjected by doctors were often inhumane and/or dangerous (J.H. Jones, 1993).

The more recent history of medical misuses and abuses of African Americans include experimentation, involuntary sterilization, and the participation of the medical establishment in the maintenance of racism and discrimination. Perhaps the most infamous episode of medical abuse of the African American community was the Tuskegee Syphilis Experiment. From 1932 to 1972, the United States Public Health Service conducted a study of syphilis, using more than 400 black male sharecroppers as their subjects. Jones (1993) book on the experiment is chilling to read. The subjects of the study were not told that they had syphilis. Some were told nothing, others were told that they had bad blood in return for free check-ups and a few other minor considerations (like lunch on the day of the checkup). The men were required to refrain from going to other doctors. They were not treated for the syphilis, since the aim of the experiment was to study the course of the illness as it progressed towards inevitable death. Antibiotics for other infections were also withheld. The subject's painful progression through the stages of syphilis was unchecked, even after the discovery of a cure. The study was not formally ended until 1972, and then only because a journalist had discovered it. Even then, some members of the medical community defended the study.

While treatments were being withheld from African American men, medical interventions were being forced upon African American women. Involuntary sterilization of African American women was legal and common for many decades and still has repercussions today (Horsburgh, 1996). In 1907, Indiana passed the world's first involuntary sterilization law, mandating sterilization of criminals, idiots, rapists, and imbeciles (Chase, 1976, p. 15). Eventually, 30 states passed similar laws, which were invoked to justify the forced sterilization of any African American that a doctor elected to label as retarded or insane. Since intelligence tests were culturally biased and African Americans had little access to education, it was particularly easy to apply the mental retardation label to African American women; African American who departed in any way from the behaviors preferred by the dominant class could easily be labeled insane. Thus, for example, 102 of the 104 sterilizations performed in South Carolina mental hospitals between 1949 and

1960 were performed on African American women (Lederer, 1996).

Legally sanctioned involuntary sterilization practice persisted well into the present-day. A 1974 federal court ruling found that 100,000 to 150,000 sterilizations had been performed over the past few years in federally funded clinics alone (Chase, 1976, p. 16).

Sterilization of African American women by the state was often effected by threats to remove welfare support. Many private doctors joined the effort to sterilize African American women by performing unnecessary hysterectomies whenever they had the opportunity. In fact, unnecessary hysterectomies were so frequently performed on low-income African American women in the south that they were called Mississippi appendectomies (Chase, 1976, p. 18).

Both court-ordered mandatory sterilizations and the routine sterilization of women without their knowledge or consent were significantly limited by legal challenges of the 1970s. However, their legacy lives on in the bodies of African American women and in the minds of public officials who conceive public policy initiatives like persuading—or forcing—mothers receiving public aid for their dependent children to submit to Norplant implantation (Horsburgh, 1996). It is not surprising that former Ku Klux Klan leader David Duke is among the politicians who have proposed the implantation of Norplant in the bodies of women on welfare (Lederer, 1996).

The legacy of forced sterilizations and the Tuskegee study continue to have repercussions today, in that their memory informs the health care decisions of many African Americans. Some activists point out that we know about the syphilis experiment and forced sterilizations only because journalists brought them to light. Only public controversy ended them. Many wonder how many other medical uses and abuses of African Americans were not uncovered and if any are still going on today. As will be discussed below, the resultant general mistrust of the medical establishment as well as specific fears about the role of the government in AIDS have seriously impacted the willingness of African Americans to seek health services or heed health warnings.

Historic African American Health Initiatives.

Just as enslaved Africans did not endure their servitude and consequent ill health passively, African Americans of the 20th century have not been passive in the face of the challenges to their health. African American women have taken the lead in this arena time and time again.

Smith's (1995) book on Black Women's Health activism covers the period from the turn of the century to 1950. Initially, the African American women's club movement began in response to the spectrum of ills facing African American communities. These women in cities and towns across the nation formed clubs, which worked to meet the many unmet needs of their communities. In time, health became a focus of their activities. The African American club of women was instrumental in the creation of Black nursing schools, hospitals, and clinics. They also directly provided health-related services (*such as education, health promotion, and disease prevention*) as volunteers.

Between 1900 and 1930, the germ theory of disease began to replace the victim-blaming theories discussed above. More out of fear of contagion than good will, members of White communities suddenly became much more eager to cooperate with and aid the African American health campaigns proposed and implemented by the Black clubwomen. The creation of the United States Public Health Services Office of Negro Health Work in 1932 can be credited to the tireless efforts of these African American women. That office served as both a clearinghouse for African American health-related activity and headquarters for the National Negro Health Movement, which lasted until 1950. While African American male medical professionals often received the public credit for the work of the movement, it was largely African American women— including both nurses and nonprofessional volunteers—in each community who did the hard work of putting the Movements programs into action in communities across the country.

African American women continued to serve as health activists and health volunteers in their local communities after the dissolution of the National Negro Health Movement. In the 1960s and 1970s, many Black feminist organizations sprang up and these were often distinguished by their emphasis on the importance of dealing with issues like health and poverty. Then, in the early 1980s, Byllye Avery sparked the formation of the National Black Women's Health Project (NBWHP), (Avery, 1990). The NBWHP is organized around the promotion of health (rather than simply the avoidance of illness) and takes a Black feminist perspective (White, 1990). As of 1990, the NBWHP had 96 self-help groups in 22 states and several overseas chapters. The NBWHP also produces educational materials, stages an annual conference attended by Black women from all over the country, and supports a variety of community health initiatives. The NBWHP is distinguished from many other health organizations by its focus on the root causes of ill health among African American women and does not hesitate to engage in anti-poverty and anti-violence efforts along with more traditional health promotion activities.

Present Limitations on African American Health

Racism and racial inequality have limited the health prospects of African Americans by limiting the economic and educational resources needed to actively pursue good health (Leffall, 1990). The poverty rate for African American families is three times that of White families and rates of health insurance coverage are low (Watson, 1993). The lack of universal health care coverage in this country disproportionately disadvantages low-income African Americans, who have particularly acute health care needs and particularly minimal access to quality health care. According to Randall (1994) the implementation of managed care is likely to have particularly negative impacts on African Americans, especially those who are low-income.

African Americans have higher mortality rates and shorter life expectancies than European Americans. The Council on Ethical and Judicial Affairs of the American Medical Association (1990) acknowledged that the underlying reasons for such racial disparities in health status include not only lack of access to health care but also differential treatment by health care providers.

The findings of the National Survey of Black Americans demonstrate that high levels of stress are associated with the challenges of being Black in the United States. Psychosocial factors such as stress contribute to health problems such as alcoholism and hypertension (Neighbors & Jackson, 1996). Thus the limitations on overall quality of life created by racial oppression can be shown to directly contribute to the health problems faced by the African American community.

In a society known to be patterned by racial discrimination, it can be difficult for an African American to assess whether a particular negative outcome is or is not the result of discrimination. Making such assessments involves a certain amount of stress. Moreover, the *perception* of discrimination causes stress, whether or not actual discrimination can be demonstrated to have occurred. Such stress also negatively impacts the health of African Americans (Mays, Coleman, & Jackson, 1996).

Another factor affecting the health of African Americans is distrust of the health care system. Fear and distrust of the health care system is a natural response to the history of experiment and abuse described above. For example, the full extent of the Tuskegee syphilis experiment was not exposed to the public until the 1970s and feelings of fear and distrust associated with this horrific episode in US medical history are still very active in African American communities (Clarke, 1996). This fear and distrust shapes the health care choices of African Americans, leading many to resist such actions as getting health care treatment, participating in medical research, signing living wills, or donating organs (Randall, 1993).

The effect of such distrust has been most acute in reference to AIDS. The medical establishment's lack of regard for the African American community can also be seen in reference to AIDS. Both factors have had deadly results.

While AIDS first gained national attention when it became prevalent among white gay men, African Americans were among the first people to die of what we now call AIDS. In the late 1970s, there was an epidemic of pneumonia among

Christine Dial-Benton, Ph. D.

injection drug users in New York City. This is now recognized as the first wave of AIDS-related deaths in the United States (Shilts, 1987). Since all of those who died were poor drug users and many were people of color, this wave of deaths was not treated as a crisis. As a result, when the next wave of deaths occurred among gay men, AIDS was tagged as a gay disease and not immediately recognized as due to a virus transmitted by blood and semen. Injection drug users—including many low-income African Americans and their sexual partners—have always been a large sub-set of AIDS patients and African American gay men have always been a large sub-set of gay men with AIDS. Thus the government's failure to act quickly with respect to the disease is more than likely related not only to anti-gay sentiment but also to racism.

At present, people of color represent the fastest growing group of people with AIDS. Black and Latino children represent over 85% of children with AIDS. The majority of women with AIDS are Black or Latino. Nonetheless, spending on research and prevention specifically targeted to the African American community has always been and continues to be insufficient.

In their distrust of the government and the medical establishment, some African American activists have suggested that the government planted HIV (the virus associated with AIDS) in African American communities and this sentiment is not uncommon in African American communities. This leads many African Americans to distrust messages about AIDS prevention that come from the government. Remembering the medical establishment's past zeal to keep African American women from reproducing, others mistrust safe sex advice coming from the medical community. Of course, failing to heed this advice can and has had deadly consequences for many African American men and women. This demonstrates the critical importance of health programs developed for and in conjunction with the African American community. AIDS prevention programs launched by or in cooperation with community leaders have a much greater chance of surmounting history in order to save lives.

Focus on African American Women

The specific needs, experiences, and attitudes of African American women are often neglected in discussions of African American health. For example, discussions of the Tuskegee Syphilis Experiment often neglect to mention the effects of the project on the wives and other partners of the men in the experiment (Gamble, 1997); they too were exposed to deadly risks as a result of the project, but they are rarely mentioned. Similarly, the syphilis experiment itself is frequently cited in discussions of African American mistreatment by the medical establishment while the sterilizations of so many African American women are rarely noted, even though the information about them is as readily available.

Progressive medical and social science researchers (e.g. Rajaram & Vinson, 1998; Freedman, 1998) argue that it is critical for health professionals to gain a better understanding of the socioeconomic factors influencing African American women's health as well as their specific health-related needs and desires. Such understanding can only be gained by putting the focus on African American women and the context in which their health problems arise.

This argument is not new. Black feminists as far back as Sojourner Truth have pointed out that African American women share some experiences of oppression with African American men and some experiences of oppression with women of all other races but cannot be simply lumped in with either group. Black women's lives are uniquely shaped by the confluence of race and gender, as well as by their own individual life experiences, and must not be asked to choose between identities (Jackson, 1973). In the arena of health, this means that Black women should be asked to get some of their health needs met by African American health programs and other health care needs met by women's health care. This is asking them to divide themselves, but in addition, the two types of programs may not add up to a program suited to the unique health needs of African American women.

The uniquely stressing circumstances faced by African American women have long been recognized by at least some scholars, as have the effects of these circumstances on African American women's health. For example, Jackson (1973) noted the particularly high rates of stress, injury due to violence, and psychological distress faced by African American women. The essays in White's (1990) *Black Women's Health Book* provide ample evidence of the many ways that the combination of racism and sexism combine to threaten the health of Black women as well as many inspiring examples of Black women rising to meet the challenges that health threats represent.

African American women involved in health activism (e.g., Avery, 1990, Davis, 1990; White, 1990) also assert that African American women's health needs will not be met simply by attending to the health challenges faced by the African American community. Neither will the health needs be met by attending to the health challenges faced by women as a whole. As noted above, the National Black Women's Health Project arose specifically in order to address the health problems that Black women face as Black women.

Present Health Problems Facing
African American Women

Black or African American women have more undetected diseases, higher disease and illness rates, and more chronic conditions (such as diabetes and hypertension) than the women of any other race in the United States (Leffall, 1990). The life expectancy of African American women in the US is five years fewer than that of white women (Blanchard & Rucker, 1995).

Heart disease is the number one killer of women in America today. Hypertension, which is a major risk factor for coronary heart disease, infringes upon the health of black women much more than it does upon the health of women of other groups. (Public Health Services, 1995). Other risk factors for cardiovascular disease are high blood cholesterol, diabetes, obesity, and smoking. African American women are more likely than any other group of women in the United States to have two or more risk factors (Greenlund, Giles, Keenan, Croft, Casper, & Matson-Koffman, 1998).

Hypertension is not only a risk factor for heart disease, but is dangerous in its own right, particularly during pregnancy. Hypertension and its sequel complicate pregnancy and can lead to pre-term labor and delivery, low birth weight, intrauterine growth retardation, abrupt placenta, and prenatal mortality (Geronimus, Andersen, & Bound, 1991, p. 393). Black women are twice as likely as white women to be hypertensive during pregnancy.

Cancer is the second leading cause of death among African American women. Black women have a 50% greater risk of breast cancer than white women (Blanchard & Rucker, 1995). The mortality rate for breast cancer is higher for black women than white (Earp, Altpeter, Mayne, & Viadro, 1995). This is, in part, because African American women are generally diagnosed with breast cancer at a later stage in the disease process (Eley, et al., 1994).

Diabetes occurs among black women twice as frequently as among other groups of women. Over 23% of black women over the age of 55 have diabetes and diabetes is the fourth leading cause of death among African American women (Rajaram & Vinson, 1998).

Infection with the Human Immunodeficiency Virus (HIV) associated with Acquired Immune Deficiency Syndrome (AIDS) among African American women has been a significant problem since the 1980s. In 1995, more than three-fourths (76 percent) of the 13,764 cases of AIDS reported among women were reported among Black and Hispanic women. In some cities, AIDS is the leading cause of death for black women between the ages of 18 and 35.

Domestic violence is a significant health problem for all women and is recognized by US cabinet member Donna Shalala as a public health emergency for women. Battering by husbands and boyfriends is a chief cause of injury and death for women in the United States. While black women are no more likely to be battered than white women, black women who are battered are less likely to utilize protective or social services for battered women (Joseph, 1997). This increases the likelihood that black women will suffer serious injury, permanent health problems, or death as a result of domestic violence.

One of the reasons that African American women often do not seek support for domestic violence is well-founded mistrust of police, social service agencies, and the medical establishment. Another reason is hesitation to name or blame black male perpetrators of domestic violence, due to internal or community pressure to maintain racial solidarity, even at the cost of their own health and safety. These have been among the issues addressed by the Black feminist movement. This movement has sought both to create new service agencies for African American survivors of sexual and domestic violence and to address the causes of violence against women in African American communities. The movement has also tried to create an atmosphere in which African American women can give priority to their own health and safety (White, 1990). The problem of domestic violence can also be indirectly addressed by the promotion of health and fitness among African American women. As White notes, women who are healthy and fit are also strong and self-confident. They are, therefore, better able to challenge abusive behavior, remove themselves from abusive situations, and physically defend themselves.

Smoking is a risk factor for cancer, cardiovascular disease, and other illnesses. Rates of smoking are unacceptably high among African American women, and this adds to the health risks discussed above. Part of the problem may be related to the prevalence of cigarette advertisements that target the black community in general and black women in particular. An often-overlooked factor associated with smoking is anger. Along with stress, African American women experience significant anger concerning the various forms of oppression they face. According to one researcher who has worked for more than ten years with women of color living in urban poverty, both stress and anger are positively correlated to smoking among African American women (Burnette, 1996).

The issue of anger brings up the issue of emotion, which is itself related to the issue of mental health. It is difficult, if not impossible, to assess the rates of mental illness among black women, for a variety of reasons. First, and perhaps most importantly, the definitions of mental illness frequently change and have in the past been explicitly racist (Kramer, Rosen, & Willis, 1973). For example, during slavery, some psychiatrists classified repeated flight from slavery as a mental illness; this diagnosis was based on the idea that people of African descent were natural slaves and that challenging that status was therefore unnatural. While the most current diagnostic standards (American Psychiatric Association, 1996) contain no such overtly biased categories or standards, it is still very possible for diagnostic bias to occur. For example, excessive anger is among the indicators of one diagnostic label. Due to any or all of the circumstances discussed above, African American women may tend to be often—and justifiably— angry (Burnette, 1996). Not understanding this, non-black mental health professionals may tend to consider black women's anger as pathological rather than normal and healthy. While research has not been performed concerning black women in particular, both race and sex have been shown to be associated with diagnostic bias. On the other hand, in part because of such biases, black women who truly are in psychological distress may avoid seeking treatment.

Thus statistics concerning mental illness among black women may include women who donut belong in them and may leave out women who do. It is impossible to know what effect this has on the accuracy of such numbers. For this reason,

I will not present statistics concerning the incidence of mental illness among black women. I will, however, note that the incidence of psychological distress is likely to be high (White, 1990). It is easy to see how the circumstances described above could lead to despair or depression. Given the incidence of violence in Black women's lives, post-traumatic stress reactions are probably often quite common. Since mental health care usage by women appears to be lowest among African American women (Padgett, Harman, Burns, & Schlesinger, 1998) many of the black women who are in such distress may not be receiving any care at all.

Factors Affecting the Health of African American Women

Social and economic repercussions of oppression and discrimination based on race, class, and sex converge in the area of African American women's health (McDonald, 1997). As McDonald demonstrates, the costs of social oppression on the basis of race, class, and sex not only directly affect the health care choices of African American women but also provoke psychosocial reactions—such as stress—, which negatively impact the health of these women. These effects can be particularly severe for Black women who are mothers. Rajaram & Vinson (1998) assert that older African American women also face especially severe health challenges, because they so often face the quadruple jeopardy

(p. 236) of chronic illness combined with social oppression on the basis of race, sex, and age.

Poverty, which affected more than a third of all African American women in 1990 (Bureau of the Census, 1992), can be shown to cause and worsen health problems among African

American women. Among the health diminishing factors faced by women living in poverty are inadequate housing, malnutrition, the stress associated with trying to make ends meet, dangerous jobs or environmentally hazardous neighborhoods, and the lack of resources for preventative health care.

Low-income African American women who are also single mothers face additional stresses that may impact health. They must make ends meet for their children as well as themselves, worry about the impact of poor housing or unsafe neighborhoods on their children, and care for the health of their children as well as their own. Increasingly estranged from the traditional extended family, urban single mothers living in poverty are particularly likely to be solely responsible for the care of their household and this stress can significantly impact their health (Sloan, Jason, & Addlesperger, 1996).

African American women living in poverty are not the only Black women without access to adequate health care. A major problem is the lack of health insurance among African American women. In 1991, only 20% of African American women in the United States were fully covered by health insurance (Yoon, Aaronson, Hartmann, Shaw, & Spalter-Roth, 1994).

African American women who are covered by medical benefits or have the economic resources to purchase health care still may avoid medical examination and treatment. In addition to the fear and distrust of the medical establishment that exists in the African American community in general, African American women have specific reasons to be mistrustful. Since the medical establishment is dominated not only by White doctors who may mistreat Black patients but also by male doctors who may mistreat female patients. According to researchers, mistrust of the medical establishment often leads

African American women to avoid visiting physicians and may decrease the likelihood that they will comply with prescribed treatment regimes (Burnette, 1996).

This mistrust may help to explain the racial difference that persists in health care usage even when factors like health insurance enrollment are controlled. For example, Padgett, Harman, Burns, & Schlesinger (1998) investigated the differences in mental health care usage between White, African American, and Hispanic women. Using controlling variables such as socioeconomic status, age, insurance coverage, and geographic region, they found that African American women were the least likely of the three groups to access mental health services in the course of a year.

Continuing racial attitudes among medical professionals represent another barrier to health care for African American women. Taylor (1999) argues that stereotyped images of African American women (i.e. matriarch, welfare mother, professional over-achiever) affect how health professionals view African American women and therefore how those professionals treat them. This helps to explain the shocking fact that 97% of obstetricians favor the sterilization of welfare mothers, who are stereo typically portrayed as African American (Horsburgh, 1996). In addition, Taylor asserts that the negative diagnostic labels that have been applied to African American women in the past continue to have an effect.

One lingering stereotype, which can be traced to the time of slavery, is that African American women do not care about their health or are passive in regard to their health. As in the slave era discussed above, reality contradicts the stereotype. Felton, Parsons, Misener, & Oldaker (1997) found no significant differences in health attitudes or self-perceived responsibility for health between African American and White young women. Gollop (1997) found that older African American women are quite active seekers of health information, who utilize a variety of resources (e.g., mass media, public libraries, etc.) to educate themselves about health problems and health-promoting behaviors.

Whether or not they hold stereotyped views, most White medical professionals have a poor understanding of the health concerns of African American women (Freedman, 1998). Freedman reports that African American women are aware of this problem and that it adds to their negative perceptions of the health care system.

The lack of access to health care has serious repercussions for African American women as a group. Their breast cancer survival rates are so low because they are diagnosed much later in the course of the disease. This is because African American women are not seen as frequently by physicians, for the reasons described above. As a result, these women are more likely to die of breast cancer.

Not all of the factors influencing African American women's health are negative. Black women have not passively endured ill health and lack of adequate health care but, instead, have created their own factors favoring health and well being for themselves and their communities. Some have done this individually, others while working in groups with other African American women. The discussion of African American women's health activism above demonstrates that stereotypes of these women as passive or unconcerned regarding health are just that—stereotypes.

Health Effects of Diet and Exercise

Regular exercise and proper diet are two examples of health-promoting activities. The World Health Organization defines health promotion as the process of enabling people to increase control over the factors of health to improve their health. Health-promoting interventions do more than protect people from disease. They are continuing behaviors to enhance the well being of an individual (Bolander, 1994).

Regular exercise is recognized as critical to physical and emotional health. As Rimmer, Rubin, & Braddock (1999) note, the health benefits of physical activity are indisputable. It is well accepted that there is a graded, inverse relationship between physical activity and all-cause mortality (p. 613). The World Health Organization and the US Department of Health and Human Services (1992) have both established the importance of exercise and proper diet as health-promoting interventions. Activities such as walking, hiking, stair-climbing, aerobic exercise, calisthenics, resistance training, jogging, running, bicycling, rowing, swimming and sports such as tennis, racquetball, soccer, basketball and touch-football are especially beneficial when performed regularly. (Duncan, Gordon, & Scott, 1991). Good dietary habits will prevent health problems such as high blood pressure, diabetes, heart disease, lung disease, breathing disorders, cancer (*breast, colon and uterus*), high cholesterol, liver disease, osteoarthritis (especially of the hips), gout, gallstones, gallbladder inflammation, blood clots, and sudden death. Each of these can be controlled by proper weight control. (Leichtberg, 1997).

Healthy individuals as well as many individuals with cardiovascular disease, including those with heart failure can improve exercise performance with training. (Adamopoulos, Coats, Brunotte, Amolda, & Meyer, 1993). Both short-term and long-term aerobic exercise training is also associated with improvements in various areas of psychological functioning. Cross-sectional studies reveal that, compared with sedentary individuals, active persons are more likely to: (1) be better adjusted; (2) perform better on tests of cognitive functioning; (3) exhibit reduced cardiovascular responses to stress; and (4) report fewer symptoms of anxiety and depression (Eysenic, Nias, & Cox, 1982).

Physical inactivity is recognized as a risk factor for coronary artery disease. Regular aerobic physical activity increases exercise capacity and plays a role in both primary and secondary prevention of cardiovascular disease (Morris & Froelicher, 1991). Exercise can help control blood lipid abnormalities, diabetes and obesity. In addition, aerobic exercise adds an independent blood pressure—lowering effect in certain hypertensive groups (Hagberg, 1990). Exercise activity can be accrued through formal training programs or leisure time physical activity (Blair, Kohl, Paffenbarger, Clark, & Cooper, 1989).

It is especially urgent that African American women take part in some type of exercise program. The comparison of heart disease mortality statistics for Caucasian and African-American women is startling. Among African-American women under the age of sixty-five, the mortality rate from heart disease is 134% higher than among Caucasian women, and 166% higher from stroke (US Department of Health and Human Services, 1992). Implementing a program of physical activity can modify the risk factors of hypertension, blood lipid imbalances, and obesity.

African American women have lower levels of physical activity and higher rates of obesity than White women (Blanchard & Rucker, 1995). Blanchard & Rucker assert that community-based fitness and health programs for African American women could modify these statistics. They suggest that such programs be located in the community, offer childcare, promote health empowerment, and provide both health education and fitness activities.

Diet and exercise are the most generally accepted areas of preventive behavior concerning hypertension. However, as Randall (1993) notes, if stress related to living in a racist society is part of the hypertension picture among African Americans, then preventive behaviors like improved diet and increased exercise may not be as helpful in the prevention and treatment of hypertension among African Americans as they are in the prevention and treatment of hypertension among European Americans. She does not dispute, however, that diet and exercise are likely to have some beneficial effects on African American health. Randall is merely noting that, given the social and economic causes of ill health in African Americans, health-promoting behaviors like exercise can only go so far; institutional change is needed in addition to individual health promotion.

Relevant Recent Research

Nies, Vollman, & Cook, (1999) utilized focus groups to identify facilitators of and barriers to exercise among African American women. They report that barriers to regular exercise include lack of childcare, lack of an exercise companion, competing responsibilities, lack of space in the home, inability to use exercise facilities at work, lack of motivation, fatigue, and unsafe neighborhood. In contrast, facilitators of regular exercise identified by the participants included a daily exercise routine, practical and convenient physical activities, personal safety, child care, weight loss, stress reduction, knowledge and commitment, enjoyment, pets, family and peer support, home and work exercise facilities, and daylight and climate conditions. The generalizability of this study is questionable because of the very small (16 subjects) sample size; however, it does indicate potentially fruitful areas for further research.

Eyler et al. (1998) used qualitative research techniques to assess patterns of activity among women of color, including African American women, over 40 years of age. While few subjects identified themselves as exercisers, most indicated that they were physically active in their daily lives. Examples of such activity included work outside the home, care giving, and housekeeping. The most common environmental barriers to exercise cited by subjects were safety, availability, and cost. The most common personal barriers to exercise cited by subjects were lack of time, health concerns, and lack of motivation.

Felton, Parsons, Misener, & Oldaker (1997) assessed health definitions, health values, and health-promoting behaviors in 62 matched pairs of black and white female college students. They found no significant racial differences in health responsibility, stress management, or exercise but did find that African American women reported significantly fewer health-promoting nutritional behaviors and less interpersonal support. Because of the youth and educational status of the population studied, the findings may not show a general picture of African American women as a whole. However, the fact that, when socioeconomic status was controlled, African American women and White women demonstrated more similarities than differences in their health behaviors is significant. This suggests that many of the racial difference in health behaviors and health outcomes may be traced to economic issues and that the economic effects of racism may be the most damaging to African American women's health.

Hahn, Teutsch, Franks, Chang, & Lloyd (1998) examined behavioral risk factors for illness and injury (e.g., sedentary lifestyle, obesity, poor diet, lack of early warning tests such as pap smears and mammography) with the aim of identifying opportunities for prevention. African American women were found to have high levels of risk factors, even when potentially confounding variables like education and family income are accounted for. They conclude that appropriately designed, culturally specific health promotion programs are needed.

Sanders (1996) identified the correlates of heath-promoting behaviors among African American and Latino women living in urban poverty. Her findings suggest that no one factor can be said to determine health-promoting behavior. A range of factors, including attitudes and beliefs about health, social support, availability of health care, quality of interactions with health care providers, and overall quality of life in the community, combine and interact with one another in their effects on health-promoting behavior. Certain environmental stressors—such as exposure to violence—appear to have particularly strong negative effects on health promotion behavior among women of color.

Maridee & Jones (1996) examined the effect of perceived barriers to and benefits of exercise on exercise behavior among older African American women. Subjects were 60-90 year old African American women recruited from urban senior citizen centers. The key perceived benefit of exercise cited by subjects was life enhancement while the chief barrier reported was lack of accessible exercise programs and equipment. A statistically significant relationship was found between perceived barriers/benefits and reported exercise.

Fennell, R. (1997) assessed the health promotion and risk behaviors of single African American students attending historically black colleges. Among males and females combines, only 33% reported participating in vigorous exercise three times per week, 37% had not participated in any sports activity in the seven days prior to the survey, 44.9% had not participated in any stretching activities in the past seven days, and 54% had not engaged in any strengthening exercise in the past seven days. Statistical analysis of these results showed that females were less likely than males to have engaged in stretching or strengthening exercises in the past seven days.

Rimmer, Rubin, & Braddock (1999) assessed patterns of physical activity among African American women with severe disabilities. Half of the subjects reported that they did not exercise, but 81.5% of those who did not exercise reported that they would like to exercise. 72% of both exercising and non-exercising subjects said that they would like to exercise more. Overall, the subjects had distressingly low levels of physical activity.

While not scholarly research, the results of a recent poll of African American women by *Essence* magazine (Kashef, 1997) are potentially relevant. Concerning regular physical exercise, 69% of respondents reported walking, 35% reported engaging in aerobics, 21% reported weight training, 13% reported cycling and 12% reported running or jogging. Since this was a relatively young and not scientifically selected sample, these figures may not be at all indicative of the exercise practices of African American women in general. However, the finding of a relationship between lack of physical activity and low health status is of interest. Of the respondents who did not exercise regularly, fully 80% reported being in fair or poor physical health and 74% reported fair or poor emotional health.

Participation in Research Projects Concerning Health

While African American women have reason to be skeptical of health-related research projects, given the history described above, they remain willing to participate in projects that are genuinely aimed at furthering the cause of Black women's health. Freedman (1998) reports that African American women remain surprisingly optimistic about the potential fruits of research and are particularly pleased when researchers seek to understand their experiences and perspectives.

This was verified in a non-academic forum when African American female readers of *Essence* magazine responded very favorably to a poll about their health practices. Many respondents thanked the magazine for asking and indicated that they appreciated that the surveyors cared enough about them to ask about their health status and health promoting practices (Kashef, 1997).

Fundamental Biological Differences in Black Female Metabolism.

In a recent article in *USA Today*, a study from Obesity Research entitled, "Black women burn calories more slowly," revealed that heavyset African American women burn fewer calories when they are sitting still than heavyset White women," (Helmrich, 1999). This phenomenon may help explain in part why African American women sometimes have a more difficult time losing weight and tend to be heavier, overall, than White women. Growing evidence suggests that White women in America may burn more calories while not engaged in any physical activity than do African American women. Nationally, about 52 percent of African American women are obese compared with 33 percent of White women. The high incidence of African American obesity has been attributed to lifestyle factors such as diet and less cultural preoccupation with thinness, but experts have wondered for years if biological factors are at work, says lead author Gary Foster, clinical director of the Weight and Eating Disorders Program at the University of Pennsylvania School of Medicine. Foster and colleagues investigated the resting metabolic rate of 122 obese White women and 44 obese African American women. The literature describes obesity as being "a disorder in which you are at least 20 percent over your normal body weight. Obesity always involves a high proportion of body fat in relation to muscle and bone. Your body needs food as a source of energy to maintain body temperature and to fuel chemical and physical functions. Food also provides raw materials for building and repairing body tissues. (American Medical Association, 1995). Although food requirements vary, even among individuals of the same height, build, age, and sex, the basic needs of most active people are about 2, 000 calories a day for women and 2, 500 for men. "However, a professional athlete or a manual laborer may need 4, 000 calories or more on days he or she is active" (American Medical Association, 1995).

Only 1 percent of people with obesity have a hormonal problem that is a cause of their weight problem. If an African American woman eats more than she need for the energy she expends, her body stores the surplus as fat. If the amount of fat becomes excessive, she meets the definition of being obese. On average, about one in every three White women in the United States are obese, compared with over half of all African American women being obese (*33 percent to 52 percent*). This very large difference in obesity patterns has been attributed to cultural preferences, lifestyles, dietary habits and the economic realities facing African American women in single-parent environments in America today.

The most obvious symptom of obesity is an increase in weight. However, not all African American women who put on weight are necessarily obese. For instance, a pregnant woman or anyone who begins to exercise after being sedentary gains weight for other reasons. But an increased amount of fat in the body tissues is the most common reason for weight gain. Obesity is associated with a wide range of serious physical disorders in African American women with many other symptoms. Overall statistics compiled by insurance companies and health organizations indicate that obesity is associated with increases in illness and death from Diabetes mellitus [a significant health concern for obese African American women], stroke, coronary artery disease, and kidney and gallbladder disorders. The more overweight an African American women is, the stronger this association becomes. The statistics suggest that if she is more than 40 percent overweight, she is twice as likely to die of coronary artery disease as a person who is not overweight. If she is 20 to 30 percent overweight, she may well be three times more likely than a person who is not overweight to die of diabetes. The risks seem higher when the excess weight is concentrated around the waist, and the ratio of the waist to the hip measurement is sometimes used to measure this risk. The definition describes the physical shape as being an important factor as well. People with a high waist-to-hip ratio are at greater risk than those whose excess fat is distributed in the hip area (Johnson, Clifford, Rifkind, Basil, Sempos, Christine, 1995)

Obesity also contributes to high blood pressure, which is itself a risk factor in both heart disease and stroke. If an African American woman has high blood pressure, she can reduce her blood pressure simply by losing weight, but the cultural influences in American society may make her reluctant to do so. Similarly, symptoms of diabetes which is a prevalent condition in African American women sometimes develops as a direct consequence of obesity and can disappear when the excess weight is lost. Finally, very obese African American women have more surgical and anesthetic complications than do those who are not obese. Childbirth for these women may also be more risky for both woman and child. Although the research indicates that African American woman themselves have alternatives with which to deal with obesity, the factors described above all contribute to keep the pounds on.

Research indicates that many overweight people find it easier to follow a sensible diet and exercise program if they do not have to do it alone. African American women would then be well advised to join a weight-loss group. Many researchers have pointed to possible fundamental differences in metabolism between Black women and their White counterparts. The American Medical Association counsels African American women who are obese to seek professional help. The research indicates that while there are anti-obesity drugs, many physicians prefer not to prescribe them because certain ones can have major adverse effects such as addiction, paranoia, and high blood pressure, which is already a problem for many obese African American women. Most people with obesity do not have a problem specifically with excess appetite. Many simply eat whether they are hungry or not. Physicians may advise them to try a support group such as Weight Watchers or, if necessary, may recommend that they seek psychological help (American Medical Association, 1995).

According to research, participants weighed an average of 224 pounds. Their findings indicate that African American women would burn an average of 1,638 calories a day if they did no activity at all. White women would burn 1,731 calories a day at rest. Susan Yanovski, director of the Obesity and Eating Disorders Program at the National Institute of Diabetes and Digestive and Kidney Diseases, studied African American and White children of normal weight and got similar findings. Yanovski says there are some intriguing theories, including possible differences in muscle metabolism. "We don't know," Foster says, but this doesn't mean African American women are doomed to be fat, they may just have to work harder" (Myer, 2000). The researchers indicated that they were directing future studies in this area in an attempt to help obese African American women and their doctors appreciate the many factors that affect weight loss). The dietary practices of African-American women have a solid foundation in the traditional foods eaten by Black women and their families in Africa, the antebellum South, continuing through to current day (Myer, 2000). This historical basis for contemporary dietary perceptions is reviewed below.

Christine Dial-Benton, Ph. D.

Historical Basis for Black Women Diets.

There is a significant relationship between contemporary perceptions of dietary habits among African-American women and the traditional foods prepared and consumed in antebellum periods. For example, studies on the adequacy of slave diets indicate that the food most slave women ate was deficient in sufficient calories and vitamins, but "compared with Latin American slavery, where the ratio of male slaves to white residents was much higher than in the United States, American slave women were well fed. Once a week each slave was issued an average ration of a peck of cornmeal, 3 to 4 pounds of salt pork or bacon, some molasses, and perhaps some sweet potatoes, The main regimen, however, was 'corn, at every meal, from day to day, and week to week" (Nash 1994 p. 370,). These vegetables were familiar to black women, since they were similar to the foods they used in meal preparation in Africa.

According to the research, African American food, also known as "soul food," is closely related to the cuisines of both Africa and the American South. African slaves brought to the New World many of their native fruits and vegetables including yams, watermelon, okra, and several varieties of beans, all of which were soon adopted into the diets of their owners. "Slaves who were taken into the plantation owner's house as cooks and other servants learned to combine their own food with the food of their masters. African American cuisine also grew out of the slaves' resourcefulness in utilizing the cast-off ingredients of the master's meals" (Myers, 2000). The creativity which modern African American women demonstrate in preparing nutritional meals for their families in many single-parent homes was also a part of the process during this period of history as well. These cooks developed methods to cook parts of the pig that was not eaten by their owner's family. They feasted on the snout, ears, feet, tail, ribs, thighs [hocks], stomach [maw], and small intestines [which when boiled and fried are known as chitterlings, or chitlins] (Meyer, 2000). This traditional aspect of modern soul food in America is an important cultural component for many African Americans. Enjoying these foods in a family environment provides a much richer experience than the mere consumption would suggest.

Certainly some of the foods enjoyed by African American families today can be traced back to West Africa. The diet there featured starchy foods such as rice and yams, both of which became important parts of the early African-American diet. Another important food then and now is rice. "Although African slaves did not introduce rice into the Americas, their experience with rice cultivation in Africa helped make possible large-scale rice production in the Carolinas and the Gulf Coast. Using both African and American cooking methods, African American slaves roasted, boiled, fried, and baked native yams and sweet potatoes" (Myers, 2000). The report notes that sweet potato pie continues to be a popular Southern dessert. These dietary components, consisting largely of starchy and fried foods are significant sources of weight increase, and their popularity among this population of Americans is pointed out as being one of the contributing causes of obesity in African-American women today. This is not to say, of course, that black American women do not eat healthy foods and ensure that their families receive a proper nutritional balance of food groups. For example, beans were also a major component of the African diet and were brought to the Americas by slaves. As in Africa, these bean varieties, including black-eyed peas, lima beans, and kidney beans, were typically simmered and flavored with a piece of meat. Another popular African import, the okra plant, was usually fried or boiled and is a principal ingredient in gumbo, a spicy Cajun dish associated with Louisiana's Creole culture that has its roots in 17th-century Africa (Myers, 2000).

In the eastern colonies the mingling of Native, Anglo, and African cultures produced a hybrid cuisine that included, among other things, barbecue. Many of the Africans who came to colonial South Carolina arrived from the West Indies, where, as linguistic evidence suggests, barbecue originated [barbecue]. Thus, enslaved Africans may have learned some culinary techniques, including barbecue, from West Indians. When cooking over a fire, American slaves began to baste their meats with sauce instead of serving it on the side, as had been the practice in Africa. Because of regional differences in livestock, "barbecue" came to mean pork in the eastern United States and beef in the western United States (Myers, 2000).

The West African tradition of cooking all edible parts of plants and animals helped the slaves to survive in the United States. Although Europeans occasionally ate the leaves of plants, slaves often prepared the leaves of plants, especially collards, by simmering them in oil, peppers, and spices. They also creatively processed and cooked corn, the food most often made available to them by their owners. From corn, slaves made corn bread, grits [bleached and hulled corn kernels], hoecakes (these are cakes of cornmeal cooked on the blade of a hoe over a flame], and hush puppies [deep-fried cornmeal with onions and spices, so-called because they were reportedly thrown to dogs around campfires in Confederate camps to keep them quiet] (Kirlin & Kirlin, 1991, p. 31).

In spite of emancipation, urbanization, and migration to the cities of the North, African Americans have preserved their foods and cooking methods. In the twentieth century, African-American foods have been produced for the mass market and many celebrated soul food restaurants have opened. Yet, according to research, African-American food and cooking methods had attracted attention early in United States history. The Black-owned and—operated restaurant Tavern in New York City was one of George Washington's favorite restaurants. Today, African American cuisine is heavily influenced by Caribbean and South American cooking, including dishes such as Jamaican jerk chicken, fried plantains, and bean dishes such as Puerto Rican habichuelas and Brazilian feijoada (Myers, 2000).

Diet Perceptions, Realities and Health Concerns for African-American Women.

In an article in the *Los Angeles Times* entitled, "Healthy Habits Cut Women's Heart Disease Up to 82 Percent," the author quotes a recent study which indicates African-American women have an "unexpectedly high ability to prevent the nation's No. 1 killer, according to a preliminary study showing that black women with the "most healthful habits cut their chances of developing heart disease by up to 82 percent" (Monmaney, 1999). Another article emphasized the correlation between being an obese African—American female and hypertension. The report, "Hypertension a greater risk for Black women," by Linda Ciampa, indicates that new research shows high blood pressure does not affect all people equally. The report says that African American women who are overweight and have high blood pressure are at greater risk than any other group for developing heart failure according to a new study. "We don't know the cause and effect at this point," said researcher Dr. Stephanie Dunlap of the University of Illinois at Chicago. "There could be a hormonal difference. It could be that when you combine these three factors together—being a woman, being African American with high blood pressure and obesity—it might turn on a certain set of genes that could dispose you to heart failure" (Ciampa, 2000). The problem of African American women diets continues to grow even as the research demonstrates increasing connections between health problems and diet in this group.

The preponderance of evidence indicates a correlation between dietary habits in African-American women and heart disease. Researchers in North Carolina analyzed data of almost 700 patients in their study, published in the Journal of the American College of Cardiology, which showed that while hypertension was the main cause of heart failure for 40 percent of African Americans, it was the cause of heart failure in just 7 percent of non-African Americans. "It was surprising to us," Dunlap said. "We've known for a long time that high blood pressure was a risk factor for developing heart failure. What we haven't known is who is at greatest risk, and now we know." Doctors said several years of uncontrolled hypertension led to heart failure in Ida Myers. Last spring, she received a heart transplant. "My doctor kept telling me to control my blood pressure, but I never knew I was at higher risk than others," she said (Ciampa, 2000).

In a study entitled, "Black-White death rates are not just a matter of health-care access," the research indicated a further link between dietary practices of black American women and heart problems. The researchers found the five-year mortality rate for African American women was 24.77 percent, compared with 18.08 percent for white women. Chelsea J. Carter reports that a study of why the breast cancer death rate is higher among African American women than among Whites suggests that unequal access to health care is only part of the explanation. According to the report, "The study was conducted at military hospitals, where supposedly everybody has the same access to treatment. Such hospitals treat members of the military and their families" (Carter, 2000). This equal access to medical care is an important consideration when evaluating statistical information concerning African American women in America today. It is important because of the disproportionate percentages that live in impoverished conditions with little or no access to adequate medical care for themselves for their families.

The research found that among the military women, the Black-White gap in the breast-cancer death rate was much smaller than it is among women in the general population. The gap still existed—Black women with breast cancer were still more likely to die than White women with the disease. It tells us that even access to health care systems doesn't diminish the gap between breast cancer in African-American women and White women, according to Dr. Barbara Wojcik, the lead researcher on the study. She is a civilian physician with the Army at Fort Sam Houston, Texas. (Carter, 2000).

A report in *Healthy Woman* indicates that African-American women are unaware of the fundamental hazards associated with their physical condition based on their perceptions of appropriate dietary practices. The report from November 1998, says that in order to explain the startlingly higher death risk for African American women, researchers looked at a number of factors in the Black female population. They found that African American women on average have higher blood pressure, cholesterol levels and more diabetes. More African-American women are also obese, a fact the researchers attribute in part to a higher tolerance for being larger (Joseph, 1998).

The researchers attempted to determine why African American women have more of the risk factors for premature death than Whites. The report notes that in the past, doctors made the natural assumption that because more Blacks lived in poverty and therefore had less money for health care, their health would naturally suffer. The report also indicates that some experts thought that because some African Americans were not as well-educated, they might not have the information they needed to eat a healthy diet or otherwise take care of medical problems (Joseph, 1998). Chief investigator Dr. Lori Mosca, a University of Michigan cardiologist, says that even when she accounted for these differences, the risk of early death fell only slightly for Black women. When she compared educated Black women to educated White women, Blacks still had a much higher risk of premature death. "When it comes to dying young, there's something about being a minority woman that we can't explain," Mosca says. "But much of it is still in their control. We know what the risk factors are, and the most important one to pay attention to is high blood pressure."

Changes in Perception of Diet in Black Women in America Today

Not all African American women are obese, and not all of them eat the same diet. While there is a preponderance of evidence which reflects that a majority of Black American women enjoy traditional dishes, *(soul food)* there is an equal amount of research which indicates this population enjoys the same foods as anyone else in the world and are as likely to pick up a Big Mac and fries as they are fried chicken and mashed potatoes. (Weeks, 1997).

While the dietary habits of the modern African American woman may not be as healthy as the healthcare community would prefer, it is clear that this population has sophisticated tastes and is becoming increasingly expansive in their tastes and cultural diversity (Carroll, 2000).

Summary of Literature Review

Throughout United States history, people of African descent have faced health problems associated with racial inequality. African Americans have been poorly served and, at times, used and abused by the health care establishment in the United States. At present, African Americans continue to face a host of health problems associated with the history and persistence of racial inequality. High stress due to financial problems and lack of access to health care are chief among the factors leading to and maintaining ill health in African American communities. The health challenges faced by African American women include both socioeconomic and psychosocial factors related to both race and gender. African American women have acted to promote their own health in a variety of individual and collective ways. However, the health promotion practices of African American women are, on average, less than optimal for a host of reasons. Exercise, which can be beneficial in preventing many of the illnesses common in African American women, is a particular area of concern. Previous research has identified some of the barriers to exercise and other health promoting behaviors but much more remains to be learned.

African American women are generally pleased to be asked about their health practices, provided that this is done in a respectful manner with the genuine aim of promoting their health.

The U.S. Department of Agriculture (USDA) has conducted food consumption surveys since the 1930's on the dietary status of Americans. However, African Americans did not take part in most of these surveys. Studies have found that perceptions of the ability to regulate health through diet and nutrient intake vary across income and race (Block and Subar,Rose, 1997).

Studies comparing dietary habits of African American women and White women often have conflicting results. For example, one study found that African Americans consume more fat than other population groups while another study found the complete opposite or not much difference (CSFII, 1994).

Method of Research

Subjects

The subjects were African American women living in a large city in the Southeastern United States. Some of the potential subjects were parents (or guardians) of students at a school, which is located in South Florida. Other subjects were participants from Norland Middle School Fitness Center, where I performed my internship. There were also subjects from the community in which I live, which is an upper-middle class area. One Hundred (100) African American women were invited to participate in the study by means of a sealed letter (Appendix A). 89 of the 100 potential subjects returned their survey. This represents a response rate of 89%, which is quite good but was less than the researcher anticipated. Of the 89 responses, 4 were incomplete. Therefore, the sample size ultimately amounted to 85 subjects. Demographic information can be inferred from the survey responses, and this will be discussed below. In summary, the subjects were 85 African American women, all of whom live in a southeastern city of the United States.

Materials

The only materials utilized were the recruitment letter (Appendix A) and the survey instrument (Appendix B). A guide to daily food choices (Appendix C) was also utilized as a guide for answering the survey. The survey instrument was constructed so as to elicit a range of direct and implicit information about the dietary habits of the subjects.

The first question asks subjects to provide their age range. Answers to this question will allow the researcher to gain a more comprehensive view of the respondent's age. The second question asks for the level of education and question #3 asks respondents for their range of income. Together, they allow the investigator to make a rough assessment of socioeconomic status and to distinguish between low and high-income subjects.

The remaining questions include a self-assessment of dietary habits, along with question #15 which ask the respondents if they feel it takes too much time to eat well.

Measures

The only measures utilized in this research are responses to the survey instrument described above and reproduced in Appendix B).

Design and Procedure

The names of potential subjects were identified through personal contact. Subjects were sent or given a letter explaining the study, along with a consent form and the survey itself. Subjects had the option of returning the survey by mail (a stamped envelope was provided) or in person. Responses were collected until a preset research deadline arrived. Survey responses were immediately separated from consent forms, which were stored separately. Analyses reported below were performed. Further analyses will be performed in the future, either on this or an expanded data set.

Survey Responses

(1).   Subjects responded to the survey concerning their *age* as follows;

18-29 15 (17.64%)
30-39 15 (17.64%)
40-49 24 (29.41%)
50-59 29 (43.11%)
60-Over 2 (2.35%)

The modal response for this statement is *__50-59.__*

(2). Responses to the statement on ***monthly income*** was as follows:

> **$999 or less** 24 (28.23%)
> **$1000-1999** 32 (37.64%)
> **$2000 or more** 29 (34.11%)

The modal response for this statement is ***$1000-1999.***

(3). Responses to the statement on ***levels of education*** submit the following;

> **High School Diploma** 23 (27.05%)
> **Some College** 21 (24.70%)
> **Bachelors Degree** 12 (14.11%)
> **Graduate Degree** 26 (30.58%)
> **PhD/M.D.** 3 (3.52%)

The modal response for this statement is ***Graduate Degree.***

(4). 8 respondents (9.41%) reported that they ***always*** eat a healthy balanced diet according to the official nutritional guidelines, 20 (23.52%) reported that they eat healthy ***most of the time,*** 39 (45.88%) reported that they eat healthy ***sometimes,*** 6 (7.06%) reported that they ***almost never*** eat healthy, and 12 (14.12%) reported that they ***never*** eat healthy.

The modal response to this statement is ***sometimes***.

(5). 3 respondents (3.53%) reported that they *always* make sure to get enough fiber and vitamins, 5 (5.88%) reported that they get enough fiber and vitamins *most of the time*, 11 (12.94%) reported that *sometimes* they get enough fiber and vitamins, 34 (40.00%) reported that they *almost never* get enough fiber and vitamins, and 32 (37.65%) reported that they *never* get enough. The modal response to this statement is ***almost never***.

(6). In surveying the statement "I drink less than the recommended amount (8 glasses) of water per day", the subjects responded as follows:

> *Always:* 34 (40.00%).
> *Most of the times*: 9 (10.58%),
> *Sometimes*: 21 (24.71%),
> *Almost Never*: 19 (22.35%),
> *Never*: 2 (2.35%),

The modal response to this statement is ***always***.

(7). Surveying the statement "I consume less than 75% of the recommended daily allowance for three or more vital Nutrients", Subjects responded as follows:

> *Always* 21 (24.71%)
> *Most of the Time* 24 (28.24%)
> *Sometimes* 23 (27.06%)

Almost Never 14 (16.47%)
Never 3 (3.53%)

The modal response to this statement is ***most of the time***.

(8). 43 (50.58%) respondents reported that their intake of some vitamins is ***always*** from traditional greens, 25 (32.47%) reported their intake as ***most of the time,*** only 5 (5.88%) reported their intake as ***sometimes,*** while 4 (5.19%) report their intake as ***almost never*** and 8 (9.41%) reported their intake as never. The modal response to this statement is ***always***.

(9). In responses to the statement "My intake of some vitamins is from fruits and sport drinks", 23 (27.06%) of respondents reported as ***always,*** 46 (54.12%) reported as ***most of the time***, 11 (12.94%) reported as ***sometimes***, 5 (5.88%) reported as ***almost never***, and 0 (0.00%) reported as ***never***.

The modal response to this statement is ***most of the time***.

(10). Responses to the statement: "I am doing all I can to achieve a healthy diet", were reported as follows; 26 (30.58%) reported as ***always***, 24 (28.24%) reported as ***most of the time***, 20 (23.52%) reported as ***sometimes***, 10 (11.76%) reported as ***almost never*** and 5 (5.88%) reported as ***never***. The modal response to this statement is ***always***.

(11). Responses to the statement; "I am very careful in selecting what I eat to achieve a balance diet", were reported as follows:

Always 22 (25.88%)
Most of the Time 26 (30.58%)
Sometimes 32 (37.65%)
Almost Never 5 (5.88%)
Never 0 (0.00%)

The modal response to this statement is ***sometimes***.

(12). Subjects responded to the statement "I pay very close attention to labels of food that I eat," by reporting 45(52.94%) as ***always***, 20(23.52%) as ***most of the time***, 7(8.23%) as ***sometimes***, 3(3.53%) as ***almost never*** and 10(11.76%) as ***never.*** The modal response to this statement is ***always***

(13). Subjects responded to the statement "Labels impact my food purchasing decision," by reporting 38 (44.70%) as ***always***, 32 (37.65%) as ***most of the time***, 5 (5.88%) as ***sometimes***, 8 (9.41%) as ***almost never*** and 2 (2.35%) as ***never.*** The modal response to this statement is ***always.***

(14). Responses to the statement "I believe that vitamin supplements are necessary to ensure proper health", were as follows:

Always 21 (24.71%)
Most of the Time 25 (29.41%)

Sometimes 29 (34.11%)
Almost Never 10 (11.76%)
Never 0 (0.00%)

The modal response to this statement is ***sometimes***.

(15). 3 subjects (3.53%) said they ***always*** feel that it takes too much time to eat well. 6 subjects (7.06%) said they feel that it takes to much time to eat well, ***most of the time.*** 31 subjects (36.47%) feel that it takes too much time to eat well ***sometimes.*** 25 subjects (29.41%) feel that it ***almost never*** takes too much time to eat well. 20 subjects (23.52%) feel that it ***never*** takes too much time to eat well. The modal response to this statement is ***sometimes***.

Tables Of Survey Results

The following tables illustrate results of the survey on
Dietary Habits of African American Women

(#1)Age Range Of Respondents In Survey
Table of Survey Results

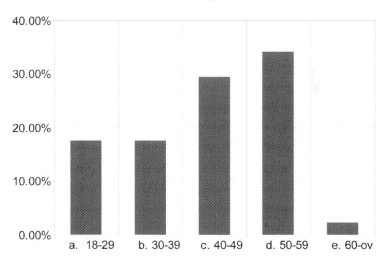

(#2) Respondents Level Of Education
Table Of Survey Results

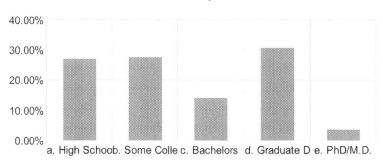

Table Of Survey Results Continue . . .

(#3) Respondents Monthly Income
Table of Survey Results

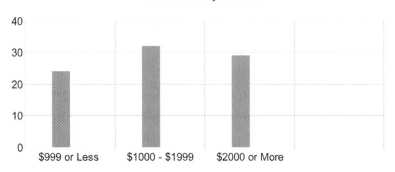

Survey Results for # 4-9

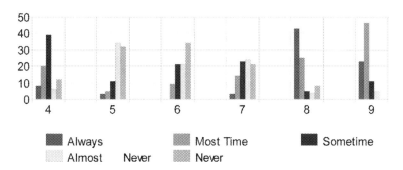

Christine Dial-Benton, Ph. D.

Table Of Survey Results Continue

Survey Results For #10-15

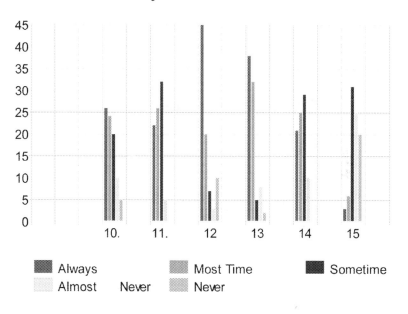

Tables A illustrate the analysis on ***always good*** to ***never good*** dietary habits from respondents by age.

Table A

Perception of African American Women

About Their Dietary Habits

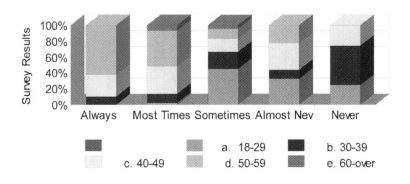

Tables B illustrate the analysis on ***always good*** to ***never good*** dietary habits from respondents by income.

Table B

Perception of African American Women

About Their Dietary Habits

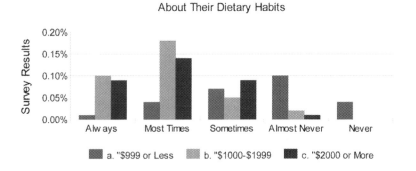

Table C illustrate the analysis on ***always good*** to ***never good*** dietary habits from respondents by educational level.

Table C

Perception of African American Women

About Their Dietary Habits

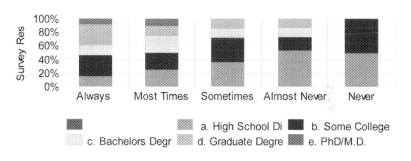

a. High School Di   b. Some College
c. Bachelors Degr   d. Graduate Degre   e. PhD/M.D.

Interpretation of findings

Discussion

In all, 55.84% of the subjects reported that they ***always*** eat a healthy balanced diet, according to the official nutritional guidelines. However, this optimistic statistic is undercut by answers on other questions. 40% of subjects reported that they ***almost never*** get enough fiber and vitamins, while 40% of subjects reported that they ***always*** drink less than the recommended amount of water per day.

On the positive side, 52.94% of subjects reported that they ***never*** or ***almost never*** consume less than 75% of the recommended daily allowance for three or more vital nutrients. On the other hand, only 30.58% of subjects reported that they are ***always*** doing all they can to achieve a healthy diet. 25.88% of subjects also reported that they are ***always*** careful in selecting what they eat to achieve a balance diet, and 44.70% of subjects reported that labels *always* impact their food purchasing decision.

52.94% of respondents reported that they *never* or *always never* feel that it takes too much time to eat well. This statistic is supported by the responses to the statement above, which deals with food labels.

Limitations of Findings

In this section, I will discuss the potential limitations of the research, which relate to the sample size and composition, the survey instrument, and the procedure.

The sample utilized was a sample of convenience based upon my access to parents of my students, to participates in a fitness center and to many of my neighbors. The first important implication is that all of the respondents were mothers (or guardians) of children. While African American mothers are an important subject, my aim was to study African American women in general.

The pool, from which this sample was drawn, was diverse in terms of socioeconomic and geographic. This was a self-selected sample, since not all of the potential subjects who were invited to participate did so. It is possible that women with a particularly strong interest in health were more likely to respond while women with a low interest in health were less likely to respond. Therefore, it may be that African American women with a strong interest in health are over-represented while African American women with a low interest in health are under-represented. This may skew the findings somewhat, at least in regard to such statement as paying very close attention to labels of food that you eat, which might be felt stronger among women with a strong interest in health and fitness.

A potentially more troubling issue concerning the self-selected nature of the sample is that subjects who's responses would be most likely to strengthen the survey might also have been least likely to return it. If in fact, a lack of time or education inhibits the health-promoting behaviors of African American women, the women most affected by this would be least likely to have the time to complete and return a health-related survey. Therefore, it is possible that the African American women who do not have the time to read the labels on the food are under-represented in the sample.

The size of the sample, while adequate, was less than ideal. I had sought a subject set of at least 100 women but was thwarted by a lower than expected response rate. In order to include the diversity of the African American female population, a sample of several hundred would be useful. A larger sample would also strengthen the validity of the statistical findings.

With a larger sample, there would be more of a possibility to utilize more demographic information, dividing the responses according to such factors as income, education, age, number of children, and presence or absence of disability or chronic health condition without creating analytic sets too small to be useful. This would involve revision of the survey instrument, in order to collect such information in a sensitive yet accurate fashion. The current instrument collects information on income, age and education.

The chief limitation of the research protocol was the method by which potential subjects were contacted. Contacting some of the subjects by sending them the survey rather than in person may have diminished their likelihood of participation. However, the only potential result of this was to diminish the sample size, and this may have been offset by an increase in response rate due to the investigator being a teacher at the school attended by many of the potential subjects children. In either case, it is unlikely that the findings were skewed in any way by the use of this protocol.

Plans for Future Research.

I consider the research study reported here to be the first phase of a longer and more complex research project. Therefore, this study might best be viewed as a pilot project. At present, the plans for future research are as follows.

I intend to revise the survey instrument in two ways: (1) the inclusion of a terminal open-ended question, the wording of which has not yet been determined; and (2) the direct collection of demographic information concerning age, income, education, and number of children living in the home.

The revised survey instrument will be distributed to a wider pool of potential subjects, utilizing a variety of strategies. For example, owners of African American owned businesses would be recruited to distribute surveys attached to stamped return envelopes. Beauty parlors and hair/nail salons frequented by African American women will be major survey distribution points. Public libraries and community centers will also serve as distribution points. At the same time as the above steps are taken or as a separate phase of the project, the Internet will be utilized to obtain survey responses from a wider geographic spectrum.

Need for Future Research.

Further research is needed in areas directly related to the question posed by this study and in the arena of African American women's health in general. Each of these will be discussed in turn.

All of the studies reviewed above concerning African American women and their dietary habits involved samples limited by age or ability. The present study includes African American mothers. A comprehensive assessment of African American women's dietary practices is needed. This should involve a nationally representative sample. Questions should be asked about different kinds of food that is eaten. The study should seek to identify the factors that promote good dietary habits as well as the factors that inhibit them. It should also analyze results not only in total but also broken down by factors such as age, income, and ability or education. Information gained about the types of food that is eaten by African American women as well as information gained about factors that promote or inhibit good dietary habits should be incorporated into new and existing health promotion programs for Black women.

The dietary habits of African American women are not yet well enough understood. More research is needed to understand the specific effects of the diet on the bodies and minds of African American women as well as the relation between dietary habits and certain diseases as they manifest in them. It is not safe to assume that such research, which has been performed on White and/or male subjects will necessarily be applicable to African American women. More research is also needed to understand how to help African American women control and manage their diet. Again, it is not safe to assume that the results of research done on other populations will apply to African American women.

Research is needed not only to assess why African American women do not eat healthy diets as frequently as they should but also seek to identify what factors would promote them to eat better. If we wish to promote good dietary habits among African American women, then we must know what the African American woman's meaning of good health is. A woman who sees healthy as synonymous with not being ill right now, may be unlikely to attend to health promotion messages, assuming that she is healthy and doesn't need to promote her health. Much more research is needed to understand how African American women think about health and diet and how a broader conception of good dietary habits might best be introduced. Methods such as open-ended interviews, focus groups, and open-ended questionnaires might be used to collect preliminary information on this important issue.

Research is also needed concerning the effectiveness of existing health promotion programs aimed at African American women. There is little information in the professional literature to indicate existing educational strategies that might be most effective in promoting dietary habits.

Another area for potentially fruitful future research concerns the attitudes, identities, and feelings of African American women who are health care activists. This substantial set of African American women is composed of women who are particularly empowered with regard to health. They appear not only to believe but also to act on the belief that they can be effective in promoting not only their own health but also the health of other African American women. It might be fruitful to learn what these women share in order to help other women to achieve a similarly empowered outlook on health.

Conclusion

The issue of African American women's health has never been more pressing than it is today. With social services cutbacks and managed health care reforms becoming increasingly popular at every level of government, there is a danger that the situation could deteriorate even further, which will leave even more African American girls and women at risk of illness and early death.

It is clear from the research that there is a perception among African American women that while their dietary habits are nutritionally adequate and relatively appropriate, they could stand some improvement. The basis for the dietary habits of African American women remain unclear, however, an intuitive analysis of the research conducted indicates that they eat what they eat because that is what they have always eaten and that is what their families have always eaten, regardless of the implications for health considerations.

In recent years, more attention has been paid to the health concerns of African American women. However, this has not been enough. Many factors combine to limit African American women's health status, access to health care, and ability to engage in health-promoting behaviors. Black women can, and are, making many of the changes within their power. However, institutional changes are also necessary. After a century of Black women's health activism, the statistics for African American women are still alarming. If African American women are to succeed in their efforts to gain and maintain good health for themselves and their communities, other Americans must begin to recognize—and act upon—the fact that every Black woman has an absolute right to be as healthy as she can be. Without societal support in the form of access to resources and changes in attitudes, health promotion behaviors such as those discussed in this research report can only go so far. We can trust that African American women will continue to individually and collectively pursue good health to the best of their ability.

Bibliography

Adamopoulos, S., Coats, A.J., Brunotte, F., Arnolda, L., & Meyer T. (1993). Physical training improves skeletal muscle metabolism in patients with chronic heart failure. *Journal of the American College of Cardiology, 21*, 1101-1106.

Alabama Department of Pubic Health. (1993). Alabama Vital Events. Montgomery, Al.

American Psychiatric Association. (1996). *Diagnostic and Statistical Manual of Mental Disorders*, 4th Ed. Washington, DC: Author.

Avery, B.Y. (1990). Breathing life into ourselves: The evolution of the National Black Women's Health Project. In E.C. White (Ed.), *The Black Women's Health Book,* pp. 4-10. Seattle: Seal Press.

Bennett, L. (1982). *Before the Mayflower: A History of Black America.* New York: Penguin.

Blair, S.N., Kohl, H.W. III, Paffenbarger, R.S. JR., Clark, D.G., & Cooper, K.H. (1989). Physical fitness and all-cause mortality: A prospective study of healthy men and women. *Journal of the American Medical Association, 262,* 2395-2401.

Blanchard, J.C. & Rucker, C.S. (1995). Community-based fitness and health training for African American women. *Public Health Reports, 110*, 207-8.

Block, Rosenberger (1988). Calories, fat and cholesterol: Intake patterns in the U.S. population by race, sex and age. American Journal of Public Health, 1150-55.

Block and Subar. (1992). "Estimates of Nutrient Intake from a Food Frequency Questionnaire." American Journal of Dietetic Assoc, 969-77.

Bolander, R. (1994). Basic Nursing: A Psychophysiology Approach, 3rd Ed. Philadelphia, Pa: Saunders.

Bureau of the Census. (1992). Statistical Abstract of the United States. US Dept of Commerce: Washington, DC.

Burnette, E. (1996, Oct.). Anger undercuts ethnic-minority women's health: Fear of racism, stress linked to poor health among ethnic-minority women. *APA Monitor.* [Online edition accessed July 1999.] Available http://www.apa.org/.

Carroll, Rebecca. (2000). "Cooking, decorating and entertaining B. Smith style," The New York Times Magazine: http://www.Africana.com, May 5, 2000.

Carter, Chelsea. (2000). Black and White death rates are not just a matter of health-care access. Metro@Augusta, [On-Line]. Available: http://augustachronicle.com/stories/040298/met.htm.

Chase, A. (1976). *The Legacy of Malthus: The Social Costs of the New Scientific Racism.* New York: Knopf.

Ciampa, Linda. (2000). "Hypertension, a greater risk for African American women." Cable News Newwork. Available Online, <http://www.cnn.com/HEALTH/women/01/Black.heart/.

Clarke, C. (1996). *The Ghost of Tuskegee.* Union, SD: TRIB.

Council on Ethical and Judicial Affairs of the American Medical Association. (1990). Black-white disparities in health care. *Journal of the American Medical Association, 263,* 2344-56.

CSFII (Continuing Survey of Food Intake by Individuals). (1994). CD Rom: Assession no. PB 96-501010, Vol. 19, Food Review, 09-21 pp. 14(6).

Derby, B. M. and Fein, S. B. (1995). Consumer use of food labels: Where are we going? Paper presented at the annual meeting of the American Dietetic Association, Orlando, Fl., Oct.1995.

Duncan, J.J., Gordon, N.F., & Scott, C.B. (1991). Women walking for health and fitness: How much is enough? *Journal of the American Medical Association, 266,* 3295-3299.

Davis, A. (1990). Sick and tired of being sick and tired: The politics of Black women's health. In E.C. White (Ed.), *The Black Women's Health Book,* pp. 18-26. Seattle: Seal Press.

Earp, J.A.L., Altpeter, M., Mayne, L., Viadro, C. I., & OMalley, M.S. (1995). The North Carolina breast cancer screening program: Foundations and design of a model for reaching older, minority and rural women. *Breast Cancer Research & Treatment, 35,* 7-22.

Eley, J.W. et al. (1994). Racial differences in survival from breast cancer: Results of the National Cancer Institute black/white cancer survival study. *Journal of the American Medical Association, 272,* 947-55.

Ethnic News-Watch@Softline **Information, Inc.** (1997) Weight Management is difficult for minority women. The Philadelphia Tribune, pp PG.

Eyler, A.A., Baker, E., Cromer, L., King, A.C., Brownson, R.C. & Donatelle, R.J. (1998). Physical activity and minority women: A qualitative study. *Health Education & Behavior, 25,* 640-652.

Eysenck, H.J., Nias D.K.B., & Cox D.N. (1982). Sport and personality. *Adv Behav Res Ther, 4,* 1-56.

Felton, G.M., Parsons, M.A., Misener, T.R., Oldaker, S. (1997). Health-promoting behaviors of Black and White college women. *Western Journal of Nursing Research, 19,* 654—666.

Fennell, R. (1997). Health behaviors of students attending historically Black colleges and universities: Results from the national college health risk behavior survey. *Journal of American College Health, 46,* 109-17.

Freedman, T. G. (1998) Why don't they come to Pike street and ask us?: Black American women's health concerns. *Social Science & Medicine, 47,* 941-947.

Gamble, V.N. (1997). The Tuskegee syphilis study and women's health. *Journal of the American Medical Women's Association, 52* (4) 7-12.

Geronimus, A.T., Andersen, H.F., & Bound, J. (1991). Differences in hypertension prevalence among U.S. Black and White women of childbearing age. *Public Health Reports, 106*(4), 393-9.

Gollop, C.J. (1997). Where have all the nice old ladies gone? Researching the health information-seeking behavior of older African American women. In Vaz, K.M. (Ed.), *Oral narrative research with Black women,* pp. 143-55. Thousand Oaks, CA : Sage.

Greenlund, K.J., Giles, W.H., Keenan, N.L., Croft, J.B., Casper, M.L., & Matson-Koffman, D. (1998). Prevalence of multiple cardiovascular disease risk factors among women in the United States, 1992 and 1995: The Behavioral Risk Factor Surveillance System. *Journal of WomenÕs Health, 7,* 1125-33.

Guthrie, J. F., C. Zizza and N. Raper. (1994). "Fruit and Vegetables: Their Importance in the American Diet." Food Review: U. S. Dept. of Agriculture. Vol. 15, pp35-39.

Hagberg, J.M. (1990). *Exercise, Fitness and Health.* Champaign, Ill: Kinetics Publishers.

Hahn R.A., Teutsch, S.M., Franks, A.L., Chang, M.H., & Lloyd, E.E. (1998). The prevalence of risk factors among women in the United States by race and age, 1992-1994: Opportunities for primary and secondary prevention. *Journal of the American Medical Women's Association, 53* (2), 96-104.

Helmrich, J. (1999) "Black women burn calories more slowly," Obesity Research in USA Today. [Online] Available: http://intl.obesityresearch.org

Horsburgh, B. (1996). Schrodinger's cat, eugenics, and the compulsory sterilization of welfare mothers: Deconstructing an old/new rhetoric and constructing the reproductive right to natality for low-income women of color. *Cardozo Law Review, 17,* 531.

Hurston, Z.N. (1990). Prescriptions of root doctors. In E.C. White (Ed.), *The Black Women's Health Book,* pp. 15-17. Seattle: Seal Press. (Originally published 1935)

Ippolito, P. M. & A. D. Mathios (1996). Information and Advertising policy: A study of fat and cholesterol consumption in the United States, 1977-1990. Bureau of Economics Staff Report, Federal Trade Commission, Washington, DC.

Jackson, J.J. (1973). Black women in a racist society. In C.V. Willie, B.M. Kramer, & B.S. Brown (Eds.), *Racism and Mental Health.* Pittsburgh: University of Pittsburgh Press.

Johnson, Clifford, Rifkind, Basil, Sempos,mChristine (1995). The National Health and Nutrition Examination Surveys. *Journal of the American Medical Association,* Vol.269, No. 23, 1995, pp. 3002-08.

Jones, F.A. (1900). Cocain habit among the Negroes. *Journal of the American Medical Association, 35,* 175.

Jones, J.H. (1993). *Bad Blood: The Tuskegee Syphilis Experiment.* New York: Free Press.

Jones, M. & Nies, M.A. (1996). The relationship of perceived benefits of and barriers to reported exercise in older African American women. *Public Health Nursing, 13*(2), 151-158.

Joseph, J. (1997). Woman battering: A comparative analysis of Black and White women. In: Kantor, G.K. & Jasinski, J.L. (Eds.) *Out of darkness: Contemporary perspectives on family violence,* pp. 161-169. Thousand Oaks, CA: Sage

Joseph, Jenifer. (1998). "Black women dying young," *Healthy Women 2000.* [On-Line]. Available: http://www.more. abcnews.go.com/sections/living/healthywoman.htm

Kashef, Z. (1997, Dec.) To your health. *Essence Magazine, pp.* 12-16.

Kirlin & Kirlin, (1991). Smithsonian Folklife Cookbook, Washington, D. C.: Smithsonian Institution Press.

Kramer, M, Rosen, B.M, & Willis, E.M. (1973). Definitions and distributions of mental disorders in a racist society. In C.V. Willie, B.M. Kramer, & B.S. Brown (Eds.), *Racism and Mental Health*. Pittsburgh: University of Pittsburgh Press.

Lederer, Susan E. (1996) Sex, race, and science: Eugenics in the deep south. *Journal of American History, 82,* 1622.

Leffall, L.D. (1990). *Health Status of Black Americans: The State of Black America.* New York, NY: National Urban League, Inc.

Leichtberg, J. M.D. (1997). The natural total health system. Printed in the United States of America.

Mays, V.M., Coleman, L.M. & Jackson, J.S. (1996). Perceived race-based discrimination, employment status, and job stress in a national sample of black women: Implications for health outcomes. *Journal of Occupational Health Psychology, 1*(3), 319-329.

McDonald, K.B. (1997). The psychosocial dimension of Black maternal health: An intersection of race, gender, and class. In: C. Herring (Ed), *African Americans and the Public Agenda: The Paradoxes of Public Policy,* pp. 68-84. Thousand Oaks, CA: Sage.

Meyers, Aaron. (2000). "Food in African American Culture," Africana.com: [Online]. Available: http://www. Africana.com

Mitchell, M.C. (1944). Health and the medical profession in the lower South. *Journal of Southern History, 10*, 424-446.

Morris, C.K., & Froelicher, V.F. (1991). Cardiovascular benefits of physical activity. *Herz, 16,* 222-236.

Murray,M.T. & Pizzorno, J.E. (1998). *Encyclopedia of Natural Medicine.* Rocklin, CA: Prima Publishing.

Nash, G. B., Jeffrey, J. R., Howe, J.R., Frederick, P. J., Davis, A. F., and Winkler, A.M. (1994). The American People: Creating a Nation and a Society, Third Edition, New York: Harper Collins College publishers.

Neighbors, H.W. & Jackson, J.S. (Eds). (1996). *Mental health in Black America.* Thousand Oaks, CA: Sage

Nies, M.A., Vollman, M., & Cook, T. (1999). African American women's experiences with physical activity in their daily lives. *Public Health Nursing, 16*(1), 23-31.

Padgett, D.K., Harman, C.P., Burns, B.J., & Schlesinger, H.J. (1998). Women and outpatient mental health services: Use by Black, Hispanic, and white women in a national insured population. In B.L. Levin & A.K. Blanch (Eds.), *Women's Mental Health Services: A Public Health Perspective*, pp. 34-54. Thousand Oaks, CA: Sage.

Public Health Service. (1995). *Health United States.* US Dept of Health and Human Services: Hyattsville, Md.

Rajaram, S.S. & Vinson V. (1998). African American women and diabetes: A sociocultural context. *Journal of Health Care for the Poor and Undeserved, 9,* 236—47.

Randall, V.R. (1993). Racist health care: Reforming an unjust health care system to meet the needs of African Americans. *Health Matrix, 3,* 127-194.

Randall, V.R. (1994). Impact of managed care organizations on ethnic Americans and undeserved populations. *Journal of Health Care for the Poor and Underserved, 5*(3) 224.

Rimmer, J.H., Rubin, S.S., & Braddock, D. (1999). Physical activity patterns of African-American women with physical disabilities. *Medicine and Science in Sports and Exercise, 31,* 613-18.

Sanders-Phillips, K. (1996). Correlates of health promotion behaviors in low-income Black women and Latinas. *American Journal of Preventive Medicine, 12*(6), 450-458.

Shilts, R. (1987). *And the Band Played On: Politics, People, and the AIDS Epidemic.* New York: St. Martins Press.

Sloan, V.J., Jason, L.A., & Addlesperger, E. (1996). Social networks among inner-city minority women. *Education, 117,* pp. 194-9.

Smith, S.L. (1995). *Sick and Tired of Being Sick and Tired: Black Women's Health Activism in America, 1890-1950.* Philadelphia: University of Pennsylvania Press.

Taylor, J.Y. (1999). Colonizing images and diagnostic labels: Oppressive mechanisms for African American women's health. *Advances in Nursing Science, 21*, 32-45.

Tippett, Katherine and Cypel, Yasmin. (1994) Survey of food intake by individuals. Nationwide Food Surveys, Rep No. 961.

US Department of Health and Human Services. (1992) *Healthy People 2000: Summary report*. Washington, DC: Author.

Watson, S.D. (1993). Health care in the inner city: Asking the right questions. *North Carolina Law Review, 71*, 1647.

Weeks, Jeffrey (1997). Values in an age of uncertainty: Interpretation. New York: W.W. Norton & Company.

White, E.C. (Ed.). (1990). *The Black Women's Health Book*. Seattle: Seal Press.

Yoon, Y., Aaronson, S., Hartmann, H., Shaw, L., & Spalter-Roth, R. (1994). *Women's Access to Health Insurance*. Washington, D.C.:InstituteforWomen's Policy Research.

APPENDICES

Appendix A
Informed Consent Form

Informed Consent Form

RE: Study of the Health and Fitness of African American Women

Dear Research Participant:

I am writing to ask you to participate in a study relating to the health and fitness of African American women. This study is conducted as part of my Ph.D. program in the area of Exercise, Health and Fitness.

The study will involve a questionnaire, which you will be asked to complete and return. The questionnaire will be designed to gather your opinion and collect your thoughts on the health and fitness of African American women. I ask that you answer all of the questions. You will be asked to give certain personal data, but this will be kept confidential and will only be used to compile total results.

If you would like to receive the results of this questionnaire or have questions about the study, please contact me at (954) 450-5927. Thank you.

Sincerely,

Christine Dial-Benton

Appendix B

Questionnaire For Survey
On Dietary Habits

Survey on Dietary Habits

_____ Questionnaire

_____ Score

Filling out this questionnaire will help me to complete an important research study. Please check one response for each statement. I really appreciate your help!

1. My age range is   _____ 18-29   _____ 30-39
                                                 _____ 40-49   _____ 50-59
                                                 _____ 60-Over

2. My level of education is
    _____ High School Diploma _____ Some College
    _____ Bachelors Degree   _____ Graduate Degree
    _____ PhD/M.D.

3. My monthly income is
    _____ $999 or Less   _____ $1000-$1999
    _____ $2000 or More

4. I eat a healthy balanced diet according to the official nutritional guidelines.
    _____ Always   _____ Sometimes
    _____ Most of the Time   _____ Almost Never
    _____ Never

5. I make sure to get enough fiber and vitamins.

_____ Always   _____ Sometimes

_____ Most of the Times   _____ Almost Never

_____ Never

6. I drink less than the recommended amount (8 glasses) of water per day.

_____ Always   _____ Sometimes

_____ Most of the Times   _____ Almost Never

_____ Never

7. I consume less than 75% of the recommended daily allowance for three or more vital Nutrients.

_____ Always   _____ Sometimes

_____ Most of the Time   _____ Almost Never

_____ Never

8. My intake of some vitamins is from traditional greens.

_____ Always   _____ Sometimes

_____ Most of the Time   _____ Almost Never

_____ Never

9. My intake of some vitamins is from fruits and sport drinks.

_____ Always   _____ Sometimes

_____ Most of the Time   _____ Almost Never

_____ Never

10. I am doing all I can to achieve a healthy diet.

_____ Always   _____ Sometimes

_____ Most of the Time   _____ Almost Never

_____ Never

11. I am very careful in selecting what I eat to achieve a balance diet.

_____ Always   _____ Sometimes

_____ Most of the Time   _____ Almost Never

_____ Never

12. I pay very close attention to labels of food that I eat.

_____ Always   _____ Sometimes

_____ Most of the Time   _____ Almost Never

_____ Never

13. Labels impact my food purchasing decisions.

_____ Always   _____ Sometimes

_____ Most of the Time   _____ Almost Never

_____ Never

14. I believe that vitamin supplements are necessary to ensure proper health.

_____ Always   _____ Sometimes

_____ Most of the Time   _____ Almost Never

_____ Never

15. I feel that it takes too much time to eat well.

    _____ Always   _____ Sometimes

    _____ Most of the Time   _____ Almost Never

    _____ Never

Thank you for your help!

Please check to make sure you did not omit any questions

Appendix C

A Guide To Daily Food Choices
(Nutritional Guidelines)

A Guide To Daily Food Choices
(Nutritional Guidelines)

Meat, Poultry, Fish
2-3 Servings

Choose lean meat, poultry without skin, fish, and dry beans and peas often. They are the choices lowest in fat.

Prepare meats in lowfat ways:

1. Trim away all the fat you can see.
2. Remove skin from poultry.
3. Broil, roast, or boil these foods instead of flying them.

Nuts and seeds are high in fat, so eat them in moderation.

Fats, Oils, & Sweets
Use Sparingly

Go easy on fats and sugars added to foods in cooking or at the table, such as butter, margarine, gravy, salad dressing, sugar, and jelly.

Choose fewer foods that are high in sugars-candy, sweet desserts, and soft drinks.

The most effective way to moderate the amount of fat and added sugars in your diet is to cut down on "extras" (foods in this group). Also choose lower fat and lower sugar foods from the other five food groups often.

Milk, Yogurt, & Cheese
2-3 Servings

Choose skim milk and nonfat yogurt often. They are lowest in fat.

1 1/2 to 2 ounces of cheese and 8 ounces of yogurt count as a serving from this group because they supply the same amount of calcium as 1 cup of milk.

Choose "part skim" or lowfat cheeses when available and lower fat milk desserts, like ice milk or frozen yogurt. Read labels.

Vegetable Group
3-5 Servings

Different types of vegetables provide different nutrients. Eat a variety.

Include dark-green leafy vegetables and legumes several times a week—they are especially good sources of vitamins and minerals.

Legumes also provide protein and can be used in place of meat

Go easy on the fat you add to vegetables at the table or doing cooking. Added spreads or toppings, such as butter, mayonnaise, and salad dressing, count as fat.

Fruit Group
2-4 Servings

Choose fresh fruits, fruit juices, and frozen, canned, or dried fruit. Go easy on fruits canned or frozen in heavy syrups and sweetened fruit juices.

Eat whole fruits often—they are higher in fiber than fruit juices.

Count only 100 percent fruit juice as fruit. Punches, ades, and most fruit drinks contain only a little juice and lots of added sugars.

Bread, Cereal, Rice, & Pasta Group
6-11 Servings

To get the fiber you need, choose several servings a day of foods made from whole grains.

Choose most often foods that are made with little fat or sugar, like bread, English muffins, rice, and pasta.

Go easy on the fat and sugars you add as spreads, seasonings or toppings.

When preparing pasta, stuffing, and sauce from pack—mixes, use only half the butter or margarine suggested, if milk or cream is called for, use lowfat milk.